This Broken Voice Will Be Heard

A Collection of Poems by Aurora Knight

Dear Reader,

Thank you so much for choosing to read my book. This has been a labor of love that has been in the works for a decade, a collection of my poetry over the course of dealing with trauma and living life when it hasn't always been what I'd imagined it would be. Everyone has a way of dealing with these disappointments and for me, it has always been writing words on a page. This project has been much like unveiling part of my soul to the world, but I am excited to be vulnerable because for so long I tried to be silent.

It is unbelievable to me how many women have experienced sexual assault and/or trauma. I have found many women over the past decade that I could relate with from this unfortunate experience. This book is dedicated to all the women who can relate to this. Our shared experiences bonded us and we could draw strength from each other from time to time. I commend their strength to be able to share with me and show me that I'm never as alone as I feel. I know that it is not just women who have experiences like I have, so to everyone else who can relate to this. I'm sorry for what you've gone through in this life. You are among the strongest people that I've ever known. I wish you peace and love in this life. I would like to encourage you that you are seen and that your voice will be heard.

- Aurora

To the Past

I know what happened to you
I see it on your face
The hurts you carry and you are
Not alone. I've felt them, I still do

Don't tell those who lie about what he did
They will only drag you further down
Tell the true ones, they'll help you
I know what they'll say, I lived it

Don't dabble into the desolate
You always are trying to be alone
The loneliness becomes your family
If you let it get too intertwined

Protect your body, it's not its fault
Breaking yourself down, will not
Lead to the healing you're looking for
I still wear your scars, faded but present

Little one, you are not at fault
You are purely enough
Dearest, everything will be okay
Let go of that hatred that you have for me

Asphyxiation

Never-ending screams haunt me at night,

Shedding the snakeskin of memories from you

 Is impossible, every time I try

To free myself from you and abscond from my

Recollections, I end up sitting in a pool of my

Subconscious and ruby tears.

I scratch away the memories until

All I can remember is the excruciating pain,

Pain from you, from myself

I wake up alone and safe, gasping

For the precious shallow pockets of air I'm allowed

For the innocence and trust I knew before you

For the touch I crave yet sends me into cardiac arrest

But memories of you have caught me in

Your stranglehold. Help me I'm drowning

In the flinches and the averted gazes as I walk by other men.

I forced you to leave me but the memories won't.

Suffering Silently

Silence is released from
My mouth freely: But
Thoughts are not so quickly
Allowed to leave my head
These thoughts swirl and
Give my body a fever

Everyone has experienced this
Fever at one point or another
But mine seems to never
Burn out entirely, making me
Obsessed over the sickness
That fills my head
The inner rage eating at me

Every so often my disorder
Will wear out my body
Shutting down.
(For a reboot, I hope)
My hate is my disorder
And it fully consumes me.

Dancing in Places I Don't Belong

As I twirl into the room,
Swirls of color flash into
My existence. Bam! Boom!
Off my feet, the bass rocks me
Into the sea of people all around,

Globs of shadows pound with
The bass, up and down, repeat
The shadows closing in over me
Suffocating me, dragging me into
Their crooked, tantalizing dances,

I sip the drink that isn't my drink
And stumble to the bathroom.
Occupied. I move upstairs to
Find another, I find him instead

I freeze. Try to run, he's found me.
He slinks over to me, I promised
I wouldn't, pressing me against
The walls of the oh too narrow
Hallway, there's no escaping this.

He pins my arms against his chest
Crap crap crap crap. Help me.
His mouth is moving, mine is not,
I can't make my legs run, why not?
He's carrying me to a room, too dark

Stay awake, stay awake, get up!
I'm too hot, want to sleep.
Mumbling nothings to me
He goes for my buttons, help me.
I'm drowning inside of myself.

No one will ever hear the words
Aching to push outside of me
Idiot, one less drink may have
Prevented all of this, just one.
Too late for that, blackness—

Wake up. Where am I?
Where are my clothes?
Who is—He's here! He—
Oh my gosh he—I run away
Vomit up my disgust and shame

I put on my smile along with my
Make-up, I dry my tears and my hair
I walk back to the room, find my purse
And as hard as I might, I simply cannot
Leave the memories to die in there.

Haunted

The face of every man
Is the same:
A reflection of their
Pants desire

Their eyes haunt me
As I try to sleep
When will I be free of
Their grasping?

Some restrain their
Hands from touching
But others feel no such
Need of propriety

To my First Love

I loved you.
For years I did.
I imagined a life for us.
As your wife with our kids.
But you couldn't stay and love me.
As your lies found our hearts.
I wanted to be free of us.
Sometimes I did.
I hated you.

*read up and down

Hands

Slide over my skin
Efficiently, detached,
They are like a phantom
I barely feel their presence

I tense up with anticipation
And fear this will not go well.
Move! Leave!
Please get away from me!

Slicing into my clothes
Searing their disgusting
Path across my skin
I shiver, leave me be.

Slut. Whore. Idiot.
Haunting my every thought
Because of a
Sad misunderstanding

I hate hands, I hate
How they feel, the
 Way they touch my skin,
I am tense and unsettled

Hands to yourself is right.
Or else what is safe?

Or sacred to oneself?
What is yours alone?

Nothing, because hands take
And steal from you,
They hurt and bleed
Your soul like a leaky faucet

Hands make breaks in security.

If I Think Too Much

As I catalogue the pressure rhythmically
Cutting into my heart, I allow myself to
Remember. The nuanced bruises striating
Outward like the cosmos, they never end.

A villain, someone I'd rather forget
Stoked the flame that altered
What my heart knew to do
I grew walls and sat inside with the graffiti

Cut up and full of slag, I realize
I'm like a neon traffic cone.
Move away. Go. Avoid this raucous
Debilitated heart

Screaming

The screaming in my mind is back.
In the background, I'm screaming.
Will anyone hear me?
I'm self-destructing on my own.
I don't know how to do this.
I don't know anything.
I don't know who can help me anymore.

Distorted

It all feels stilted
Twisted in view
Nothing I say
Will change the ache
Of wrong stifling me.
Did I do something?
What did I do?
Is it my fault?
I'm terrified
Please don't leave me
Please don't leave me
Please don't leave me

Floating

My thoughts come in waves
Crashing through my skull,
Beating me up from the inside,
Disorienting and painful

I am a zombie, stumbling
Through my days silently,
Wishing for a sleep that just
 Will not present itself to me

These days my eyes glaze
Over from the stares I get,
I no longer care anymore,
Leave me in peace, I float.

I'll come out on the other side,
Maybe you won't recognize
The girl who I'll become,
Maybe I'll lose you too

For now I am comfortable
In my black garments, staying
Safely blank, a new slate
Waiting to be corrupted by
The world's wishes for me

As I float along the rivers of life,
The waves guide me along,

Sometimes I crash into the rocks
And other waves are oh so gentle

My life feels like an endless dream,
Nothing I do feels real anymore,
Can a doctor do a brain transplant?
The solution to this floating is
Nowhere to be found…

Fading Away

After the storm it all looked different, the dismal overcast
refused to leave with its watery companion, making a point
to dangle over me like a noose. I stare out of the windows to
my soul, blackened in respect for my shrinking reality.
Seeing the sunlight, the flowering pinks and purples outside
of me only serves as a cruel and ostentatious reminder of
my own grievous state. The water stains linger black and
brutal against my ashen face, reminding me of my losses. In
the season of rebirth and color, my world darkened and died.

Running

Pound, pound, pound
My feet push off the ground
As I continue to run
The red flags fade into black

In, out, in, out
My breathing is shallower
The force I push into my lungs
Rips out of my lips in puffs

Everything burns, burns, burns
My muscles, my eyes, my heart
I'm leaking out all of the things
I tried to hide away, seeping into my clothes

As I run away from everyone and everything
I enjoy the radio noise that threatens to overtake me.
Overwhelms my senses until I can no
Longer feel anything, numbness sets my bones

Don't you see? I run away
From the troubles I find
From the tears I refuse to let fall
From the reminders of you
From the silence that makes my ears ache
From the smell that sweetly chokes me
From the truth, I run

The truth of how much I miss you
Of how much I wish I could join you
In your eternal sleep,
I'm so close to sleeping forever
But my eyelids open slightly just to run

I cannot survive with the burning in my throat
If it's not from alcohol,
I cannot survive with laughter in my eyes
If it's not faked,
I cannot survive with a smile on my lips
If it's not from lack of sleep
I cannot survive being hugged
If I can no longer feel your arms around me

I simply cannot exist if you are gone

Anxiety

Hands clawing up through my
Stomach into the valves of my
Heart and onwards to my
Lungs, grabbing any breath I have left
The lack of oxygen stalls my
Brain, making any movement
Impossible, any thought frozen
Any reason incapable.
Stuck in place.

Stormy seas in my stomach, rumbling, tumbling
Churning away, in hopes that you'll see my breakfast
From yesterday (I couldn't eat this morning)
A shard of glass that imbeds into my heart
The thing about glass is…
Once it breaks it shatters into so many pieces
They delve into my bloodstream to travel to my
Back and shoulders
My body is in chaos and my mind is
Blank.

Sometimes

Sometimes the heat from your body
Excites me, filling me with joy
Others, that same heat haunts me
Entering my dreams unbidden
Reminding me of another place
Where I was filled up in terror

My Eyes

I went days staring into a mirror
Not for Vanity's sake
I looked into the windows to my soul
Searching the abyss of my pupils
Every day I stared
Looking for something I could not find
Not in the black hole or the rings of
Dirt slowly getting sucked into it
I searched desperately for a light
Every day going slightly madder
Trying to find the light of my soul
My fighting spirit, a savior where
There no longer was one.

Don't Tell Me

Don't tell me you love me
Never dare even whisper it
Putting the thought into the air
Like a dandelion's wishing fluff

Don't tell me you miss me
Keep your promises for some
Lonely girl who will willingly twirl
Herself around your crooked finger

Don't tell me you want me
Just like you thirst after success,
Blinded by the insatiable need
To possess what is not yet yours

Don't tell me that I'm yours
Like Destiny herself declared that
My heart will only ever belong to you
When the future is so uncertain

Don't tell me anything at all.

To the (un)lovables

It begins with a whisper
Into your heart or ear
From a love you once had
"you are not enough"

the whispers become a symphony
the soundtrack to your love life
omnipresent voices saying
"no one will truly love you"

To silence the band you give in
Let him use pretty empty words
And passionate need to tell you
"I will be the only one to love you"

but the beat hasn't changed
and your heart knows the song
it soon notices the (un)truth as well
"you can't be loved ever"

you fight the music
screaming, drowning in rage
you shout the only hope left
"No one is unlovable"

Not even you.

The Sweet Darkness

People want to be lighthearted
As though if we see them as light
It will erase their darkened scars
And midnight nightmares

But I want them to see me as pitch
So, if anyone sees a glimmer
They should know not to expect
A ray of sunshine, but rather
A thunderstorm instead

Beware the Lightning.

Scary Love

Bonds between two people
Strong enough to overcome all
Helping each other stay tall
How can anyone commit to that?

Feigning apathy for you
Is the defense I choose
I need to stop this, and will.
Is it too late for that?

Maybe if I chase you away
Share my worst (inside I've died)
Then you'll tell me good-bye
But don't dare hug ever me

As long as you continue this
Persistence, you've infected my
Body, mind and soul (is it too late?)
Do you see that?

The only option is to run
Flee from the sweet kisses
You plant on me. (I can't stay here)
I miss you, do you miss me?

Sorry my love, I can
Not break my chains for you
But you give me hope (is it too late?)

Are you ready to try?

I do not promise smooth
Cruising, I only know fighting
Running, kicking and screaming
Can you deal with that?

I love you. I will admit to that
This is a scary love,
An impossible love.
So why do I want this to work so bad?

Grief

Five to Seven Stages
Do they always go in order?
Can I go backwards?
What if I was angry before I was numb?
I go through so many emotions each day
First I'm numb, then I'm crying,
Then I'm angry, and then I'm guilty.
I feel it all. I want to feel it all.
Unless, I don't.
Then I want none of it.
Is it possible to go through everything in a week?
How deeply can I grieve to speed up the process?
If I lock myself in my room for days, will I emerge
Completely free from grief?
Or is that just another stage, believing that I am
Finally free from grief when it isn't done with me?

Forgiveness is a Curse

No sé como perdonarte[1]
I am all by myself,
The mess that is you confines me
Lo unico que se es mi odio por ti[2]

I am all by myself,
Everyone sees it in me but
Lo unico que se es mi odio por ti[2]
My life is consumed by it

Everyone sees it in me but
They ignore me just the same
My life is consumed by it
Enciendo mi odio aun más[3]

They ignore me just the same
As I try to ignore you but can't
Enciendo mi odio aun más[3]
Even though you apologize

As I try to ignore you but can't,
After all the mess that is you,
Even though you apologize,

No sé como perdonarte[1]

[1]: I don't know how to forgive you

[2]: The only thing I know is my hatred for you

[3]: igniting my hatred even more

Wrestling with God

Father, do You see me?
Adonai, do You still care for me?
Jehovah Rapha, are You still there?

Here I am Lord, I am kneeling at Your feet
As Your daughter, I am trying to trust You
But tonight, it is nearly impossible

Why, Jehovah Jireh, do You allow for
All this pain to continue plaguing me?
What is the purpose to it now?

My Qanna Lord, why did You let it
Happen in the first place?
Why did You allow it to happen to me?

Better me than another, I've always told
Myself, better I hold this hurt than push it
Onto someone less capable of holding it

However, Jehovah Shabuoth, after all this time
I still am at a loss for how my pain could
Be used for Your glory. Where is the glory in it?

Lord, You have plans for me that I am unaware of
You created this world, and have saved this world
You can heal the wounds I feel so sharply today

My question is: Will You take them away?
Or will You let them remain inside of me?

I Remember Everything

I remember the clothes
I wore as your hands
Roamed underneath them

I remember the feel
Of you tugging me closer
And closer to your body

I remember the terror
Preventing me from
Speaking or moving

I remember the tight
Closing of my throat, my
Body warning me of tears

I remember the way
You pulled at my wrist
Wanting to go to another
Place to continue what you started

I remember the laughter
Grating my ears
While I'd cry that night

I remember every
Painful moment after this one
Where I hurt me to block out

How you hurt me

I remember the names
They called me, the
Questions they asked me

I remember the others
I used after to try and
Escape the terror

I remember the nightmares
Ones that still come
To haunt and remind me

I remember seeing you
Wanting you to see I was fine
And even beautiful

I remember every guy
After you trying to understand
Why I am how I am

I remember the hiding
And crying every time
I was triggered

I remember constantly feeling
Alone, broken, destroyed
The years it's been

And I doubt you
Remember anything

To the Little Girl Inside Me

Hello, Little One
I'm surprised to see you today
It's been so long since we've
Had one of our conversations
(I haven't missed them one bit)

Usually they start with your
Temper. quickly rising and insistent.
You scream. No. Stop. Bad. Slut.
Your indignation is quite apparent
(because you know better now)

Your small fists rise up and
Repeatedly swing at me until
I can no longer ignore you
You demand to be heard.
(because you were not heard before)

Oh, Little One
How my heart breaks for you
With your tear-streaked face
Your wild eyes and a body
Marred by scarlet scratches
(because you wanted his memory gone)

Oh, Little One
These memories are mine as well
These nightmares are shared

The fear, you so intensely feel, too
(Me too, Little One)

My dear, with all that hatred
You've locked away, the shame
That you refuse to let go of
You are choking me out
(because I want to let it go)

I'm tired of talking you down,
Of letting you out when we're alone,
Of letting you decide what is enough
I'm tired of our conversations
(because I want to let you go)

So, My Little One
Will you stop fighting so fiercely?
Will you admit that we're safe now?
Will you put down your fists for me?
(because I'm tired of losing to you)

Confused Little One,
You took the words they said about us
And latched on too tightly
You cling to them in hopes that
It will make sense of the senseless
(because they were supposed to help us)

Remember Little One,
How I carried you and deferred

All decisions to you?
Remember how I sat up with you
As you cried? How I held you?
(because no one else was allowed to)

Little One,
I love you. I am so proud of you
For the way you've protected us.
For the way you've defended us.
I am so grateful that you remember
(when I often choose to forget)

But, Little One
We are not twelve anymore
We are not weak anymore
We are not broken anymore
We are not ignored anymore
We have overcome so much

Can we just celebrate that instead?
Can we stop fighting each other?

Before

Before you, walls were my solace
Before you, locking myself in was a privilege
Before you, I could stand the loneliness

But you came and went looking for me

And with you, I was trapped by walls
And with you, my keys were necessary
And with you, the loneliness was cold and unfair

I bled from the force I used breaking out of there

Yet you only saw walls you wanted to tear down
Yet you never saw a challenge you wouldn't face
Yet you liked the all encompassing savior complex

My walls were obliterated but so did the challenge I posed

After you, my walls are my nuclear family
After you, my jail is my sanctuary
After you, I can't bear to break out again

Stone by stone I will rebuild again
I am sinking again, to the depths of my privacy
Because before us, I was never afraid of trespassers

Completely Gone

I think of you.
It makes me think of how much I am lost.
Not lost to you.
But lost the ability to love.
Love has broken up
It has given up, and beaten me
It has cried out,
Refused to eat or sleep, love has
Pummeled me.
But here I am considering:
If I love you,
Will you choose to stay?
If I love you,
Will you love me too?
Do I love you
Or just thoughts of you and I?
When is it time
To just give in and accept the fall?
And how do you know
When love is completely gone?

I will learn

Someday I will learn to give in
To you and your warm eyes
To your safe and strong arms
To your smile and the words you say.
Right now, I am a fortress crumbling
To your feet, you're walking around
My walls waiting to sound the
Trumpets, so that I will let you in,
And I'm inside knowing that you are
Coming for me, finally.
I thought I didn't need a prince
Because I am not a damsel in distress
But I am distressing over the
Possibility that you will unlock the
Chains that keep me secure in
My tower, away from you.
But know that
Someday I will learn to give in.

Do You Have Any Answers For Me?

God, why does the world rage like it does?
You have such power to make it all stop
To make everything stop
And yet you allow it all to continue and persist
The horrors. The fear. The way the world seems to get
worse.
I know there's hope too, where people band together and try
to do better.

God, I don't have answers and I know that the only answer I
need is that You are God
and that You've got this.

People are dying, people are sick, people are being killed
because of the color of their skin. God, does humanity never
learn? Do we always slowly get worse?
Is life always supposed to be this confusing and messy? I'm
not sure. I'm not sure. I just know that some days, I'm more
than ready to come home. And I'm reminded that THIS is not
home to me. That there is something better that is better.
That is right, with no fear or tears or screaming that rings
through the night.

God, why do the nations keep finding ways to kill each other
over silly things?

I know that to stop it you would be changing the foundation
of your creations. That we would not be free. That we would

be enslaved or gone. Some days that feels so much better than watching the pain that goes on in the world.

Heaven is going to be better. This is not my home. This is not my home.

Patchwork

I've decided to go back to the start
And patch up all the missing pieces
That have long left my heart

We fit like puzzle pieces jammed
Into impossible places by a
Child refusing to accept the truth

What I thought to be love
Was a useless addiction
Because I loved being in a pair

Like a rubber band we split apart
Only to be brought together
By an unhealthy sting of attraction

Where he went I trailed along
Until I woke up one morning
Without a sense of belonging

I needed someone to fill the seams
Where I couldn't love me
Instead he just ripped me apart…

Playing Games

Tried to convince me, you did not succeed
Still your voice called out to me, lies they were
I knew through it all, you were consumed by greed
Women were your addiction, and I wasn't the cure
I ignored the warnings burned into me
At first your love was so overwhelming
But my tolerance died when I dared see
The extent of your lies and meddling
Soon as I made you leave I was bitter
Anger welled up inside of me, hatred
Became my remedy, my love killer
Taking away the one thing that's sacred
So I locked far away my love from you
Hoping that my heart could be locked up too

Poisonous

Why are we stuck?
There's a constant mix of
Heartache and headaches because
Of the cycles of love
We seem to be caught in
I love you only to hate you

The beginning is beautiful
Nothing compares to us but
Us together is like a sunrise,
Every day we are forced to
Start over from scratch

I cry in despair then to
You for comfort because
I'm so lost and have no
Where else to turn and
I can't help myself when I
Look into the warmth of your arms

~~Broken~~

The words coming out of your mouth
Have this uncanny tendency to
Pick up an ice pick and tap at my heart

The tears that streak my face are met
With your frosty countenance
Devoid of any sympathy or grace

I searched for comfort in all
But fell to my knees
Alone, shattered, and you gone

The days where I seek your face
In the crowds are when
I forget to remember what you said

About how I am broken, ruined
Tainted, damaged and
Somehow less than worthy

The times I remember how you feel
Remind me that no one
Should have the power to brand me,
Calling me crushed while I am still healing

To the One (I miss)

It's taken me some time to catch up
To the reality you've been seeing for a while now
There is an undeniable bond that connects us
You are the hardest to say goodbye to
Because no matter how much time passes
You are still the one (I miss)

I tried to be without you in my life and yet
Here I am, returned with a crack or two
And several nicely healing scars,
Staring at you like I've only just found you
Because no matter how much times passes
You are still the one (I love)

But every time I come to all these conclusions
I end up leaving, since I'm a dream-chaser
I like to be on the move, never stuck for long
Please hold onto the memories and pictures
Because no matter how much time passes
You are still the one (I miss)

Put 'em in Your Pocket

Catch me I'm falling
Like a star,
Burning the whole way down

Everyone's standing by
Wishing on me to crash
To the ground

Someday you'll all look up at
The place I used to be and see
The remnants of the light I used to hold

Help me relieve gravity
And regain my place
As part of the galaxy

Unite me with my constellation
The only home I have left
In this ever expanding universe

Trauma

This feeling that overcomes me where I can feel everyone in
the room
Not that they are looking at me or see me
But I am acutely aware of where everyone is
Where their hands are.
Where they are standing.
How close are they to me?
How much distance is safe enough?

This feeling where I genuinely can't tell if I'm excited
standing so close to you
Or if I'm nervous and about to be triggered by your hands on
my waist
Getting distracted because I want to avoid remembering
But remembering anyways because I'm trying not to
Being closed off to you
Because I have to for a second
So, I can breathe

This feeling where fear is so much a part of intimacy for me
That I have fantasized about people hurting me, using me
Because I think that's what sex should look like, someone
taking from you
I am terrified of soft, sweet caresses. Of being cherished
Since they are so alien to me
Since I don't think I should have that
That I'm not meant for that type of love

This feeling where I can't focus on what you are whispering
to me
Because my body is screaming at me to put more space
between us
But I ask you to repeat what you said again, to be polite
And I try to ignore my body
With its screeches that I am in danger
Because I don't want to make you feel uncomfortable

This feeling where I want him to see me as beautiful, years
after
Because I somehow think his opinion of me means anything
That I need his approval
That I need to win somehow
That I need him to recognize me
But not see all the ways he hurt me

This feeling that comes with the nightmares
Waking up, disoriented, with recollections of someone
Who wanted to hurt me, someone who wanted to use me,
To make me their pet. Where I feel like I can't escape
All these feelings because even my mind
Is out to get me

This feeling where I know that I am not to blame, but the
shame eats me
It tells me that I am not good enough
That no one will want me
or that if they do, it's only because they don't see me
Where I remember all the lies they told me

But I can't see where truth is anymore

This feeling where I am so angry that I can barely breathe
At my dad, for kissing me on the forehead when he gets
home
All the times where a hug made my insides turn out
When I couldn't trust someone only wanted what they said
Because they always want more
They expect more. They demand it.

This is how my trauma presents.
Not many people see this.

Sleep Deprived
I'm tired of thinking of you
But my mind won't stay quiet
I can manage in the day
Focusing on the tiny pieces of life
But at night I am cursed with dreams
Of you and me
Saying we're together with kids
And a white picket fence
But I wake up to the emptiness of
My bed
I'm tired of wanting what I can't have

You Have to Keep Moving

A girl. Sits.
Her knees are bent underneath her.
She sits on the side of a gravel road.
Tears blur her vision and
She cries.
Her arms are wrapped around her waist and
she frees one to trap the cries
Escaping her mouth
She shakes. Quakes. Trembles.
Her hands reach out to hold something
Anything. Something.
But There is only gravel, which slips through her fingers
She stretches out until she is practically bowing on the rocks
And she whispers...
"Daddy, help me"
"Please help me, I can't do this"

Silence.

She brings her hands to her chest.
She releases the rocks and
Looks up.
Uses her dusty hands to wipe her face free of tears
Looks forward. Eyes empty.
She isn't crying anymore.
She pushes herself to her feet,
Leaves the dust on her knees
But dusts off her hands

At first, she only takes a few steps.
Then she pauses.
Looks down, then back.
But she turns forward.
Takes a deep breath. Shoulders back.
A small smile graces her face.
Fading slowly as she makes her way down the road.
Alone. But moving.

And utterly
Silent.

If You Leave

I didn't know that I had the ability to love at all
Let alone, the love that I have for you
Which the oceans depths cannot compete with

In case you leave me,
I will convince myself that the scar you'll
Leave behind will not etch my insides too deeply,
Merely surface wounds that burn like paper cuts

However it's in the heaviness in my chest
An unfamiliar, yet familiar weight
That belongs to you alone
Tells me your memory will stay with me (even if you go)

If you left, I wouldn't blame you,
If not, you might burn out from loving me
I wouldn't wish that on anyone, let alone you

The pain in my heart tells me that
I must prepare for the worst
For the day you leave me all alone
Nothing is certain is the certainty I live with

So if you are just going to leave me
Can we cut to the chase?

How?
How am I to do this?
Oh, how I want to.
I really want to.
But sometimes I just
Can't.
Can't eat.
Can't sleep.
Can't hardly think.
Baby, I'm breaking.
And all the memories
Are overtaking me.
How you love me.
How you want me.
How you need me.
Can't be without me.
Can't love anyone else.
Can't get any better than me.
And yet.
There was one day where
Those were lies.
Where you didn't love me.
Didn't want me.
Didn't need me.
You could be without me.
You could love someone else.
You could have better than me.
And you took it.
How I wished you didn't.
How I hoped you hadn't.

How I trusted you wouldn't.
Didn't expect that.
Didn't want to hear it.
And yet.
It happened, and I know it
I can't escape it
And I love you anyways.

Baby, I'm breaking.

I Beg For Sleep

Another night where I sit with my back against my bed
Sitting on the floor with my knees tucked to my chest
Arms wrapped around them
I am crying.
My chest feels tight
A sharp pain slightly left of center
My hands ball up and I press
Them to that painful spot
Hoping it stops. Just stops.
Suddenly, I'm sobbing.
My hands fly to my mouth
Stifling the sound so others can sleep tonight
Not me.
Tears are hot as they run down
My face.
Snot is coming along too.
I arch my back and fall over.
One hand on my chest, the other on my mouth.
Then I go silent again.
My hands wrap around me.
Around my knees, my waist, my throat, my hair, my head
Wherever I need to to quell the pain
My mouth opens.
And I'm screaming.
I'm screaming.
I'm screaming.
But it's silent.
Since people are sleeping.

So I bite my arm to stifle the sounds
And I rock back and forth
Rocking, crying, screaming.
And I mouth "Daddy, help me"
"Daddy, I can't do this"
Over and over again.
It's hours now.
My head is fuzzy, delirious in its grief
My temples ache.
And I crawl into bed
Silent, yet still crying.
Tossing and turning but,

Finally, I sleep.

Avoiding

More nights keep passing
Where I stay up late to avoid sleeping
I can't sleep.
I haven't been sleeping since then.
Hoping that exhaustion will take me away.
I'm running.
Trying to burn myself out
So there's no energy left to cry.
I'm failing.
I keep thinking of you in everything I do
And I know I need to be forgetting everything.
I don't want to.
I want to hold onto it all, every moment.
The beautiful chaos and the incandescent pain
But I let go.
Because I should. Because I have to. Because I need to.
Because holding on makes everything worse.
I
Let
Go.

To the Man I Left

I'm sorry.
I didn't realize that my baggage
Could drag me down like that
I didn't realize that my scars
Would run like the Earth's rivers
Forgive me?
I wanted to ignore the flashing
Yellows my heart was beating out
But instead they replaced all
Sweetness with doubt and lies
I miss you.
I hate my cursed heart
I hate the handprints leftover from others
That I can't seem to erase from my body
Like tattoos, a cover up is my only option
I miss you.
I was like the lunar phases
Open with my love like a full moon
Then slowly pulling away until
My love was nothing, but it returned
Forgive me?
If you do exonerate my indiscretions
Will you be like the sea's tides
Pulled closer by the force of my gravity
Or will you be lost at sea to me?
I'm sorry.

The End of the Night

I climb the steps
Dragging my toes on each one
They're heavy. My feet.
Open the door that always creaks
And move into my room.
It's dark, the shades drawn.
No lights tonight.
Maybe a candle or two.
I look at my bed and
know that I won't be sleeping tonight (like others)
The door closes and my head rests on the back of the door
My face crumbles.

Finally, don't have to hold it in anymore

I sink to the floor with my back against the door
Tears streaming down my face.
I crawl to the pile of clothes
I haven't put away in days
Clean, but messy.
And I lie down.
I drag the covers of the bed
Pull them over my head
And I lie there.
Comforted by the darkness.
Hoping that if I sink into the floors
No one will find me

And I can pretend to not be hurting
When I am

I close my eyes against the tears.
Deep breaths.
My mind is racing
I am so very tired, but I can't stop
All the thinking
I tuck my knees to my chest.
And I lay there until
I let myself move from the floor
To my bed
Where I still just lay there.
Remembering what I can't forget.
Feeling my pillow dampen
And waiting to see if I'll finally sleep tonight
(or see the sunrise, whatever is first)

Unfinished Poem #83

You lost yourself, but I lost part of me to you
It scared me at times, knowing the lengths I would go for you
How deeply I wanted to make you happy
How much love I wanted to pour into you
At times I was hesitate, resistant. Afraid.
But you made me feel safe. And so, I climbed aboard this
sinking ship
Because as long as we were together
I felt like I was floating, and I couldn't sense water slowly
rising
Do we eventually feel weightless when we're drowning?

Albums

Lovely days with you
Become photographs
Ingrained in my memories
I pull them out almost daily
Your smile calms me and
Drowns me because you are
Only found in albums now.

List of things that have made me cry:
A tub of pineapple coconut ice cream.
My birthday card.
A rom-com movie.
Old text messages.
The first time I saw you.
When you didn't reply.
Being asked how I am.
Sad songs and
Love songs alike.
A movie you hate.
Being close to your house.
Passing where you wanted us to live.
Being where we met.
My tattoo.
My old house.
Your unsent birthday presents.
Lots and lots of pictures.
Talking about the future.

Forests in My Mind

One of these days
This girl who hurts
Takes an axe
And swings
And swings
And swings.
She cuts through part of the tree
In a fury, a rage fuels her
She screams and releases some of the tension inside her
But then it grows as she tires
She looks at the tree and knows
She has to finish cutting it down
She curses the tree, chanting it in her mind
Her swings are erratic, like her pulse
And she doesn't care
Her only need to to take down this tree
It is her enemy and she must take it down
Her breathing is heavy and her eyes slightly wild
She breathes out when it falls
Looks for the next one.
And she swings
And swings
And swings.
This tree whose only offense is growing in the wrong spot
Halfway through the second tree,
She pauses

Her voice breaks as she says
The tree didn't do anything wrong
It just had to sit there and take it
This tree who didn't choose it's spot to be planted
It grew in the wrong spot
And it's destined to get burned
She apologizes to the tree and thanks it for its help today
She puts her palm to the bark before backing away and she
Picks up the axe
And swings
And swings
And swings.
The third tree was done with a cold, vicious swiftness
There was no remorse, no screaming
Her swings are steady and her rhythm is consistent
The only sound left in her ears
Just the quiet grunts from concentrated efforts
A focused attack on the tree.
It falls
They all fall.

I'm Busy

I've been trying to stop thinking so much lately.
Just have a few days where I can escape the thoughts that
have been swarming me.
Surrounding myself with tasks and people and noise.
Staying up late to avoid time to myself
Time to think about you and all the things we were.
Time to think about how you hurt me. How it still hurts.
It's been relieving to not think.
It's been relieving to laugh.
To do anything that has absolutely nothing to do with you,
To not talk about you and pretend you don't exist.
But you're still there.
And I can't tell if the good or the bad memories
Are more haunting.

If I Start the Tears Falling

If I start the tears falling
There shall be rain tonight
Enough to stop the fires
From spreading
Flooding my mind with grief
Instead of pain.
Which is easier to bear?
Constant pain searing it's
Message into my heart
With every tic of the clock
Or these shots of grief that
Rob me of thought and will
To remove the cement
Sealing me into the memoriam?
Which one can you live with?

Run.

Run until you can finally breathe again.
Run until the world makes sense again.
Run, Run, Run, dear girl.
When you stop, you'll fall.

Freedom

Sometimes I wish I could forget
The times I curled up in my bed alone,
Tears tearing away any self –respect,
And my heart becoming petrified stone.
The darkest of my secrets were kept by
My pillowcase, recording tears at night,
While during the day I doled out lies.
I tried to keep my face straight with pure might,
But you saw me bereft of my magic show,
All my secrets shattering around you,
Because of your gentle query, I know
Finally, after the tears, I will do
What I should have done many years ago
And like birds in migration, let my lies go

Crashing to Reality

Before the dam was torn down
Nothing came out
Not a leak of emotion
Not a spray of tears
Nothing escaped my walls.
Now I am the one who can't escape
The waters crush me
Wave after wave
Drowning me daily
Each one big enough to
Push me down, to drown out
My reason, my light
I'm clinging to this rock I call
An island
Hoping for, praying for the strength
To survive this storm

Please Stand

You sit in the darkness wondering where we went wrong
What you messed up and how you let this happen to us
You sit in the darkness and sleep on the floor
The scratchy carpet feels better than the haunted bed
You sit in darkness and learn to love it because everything
Feels heavy and hopeless and wrong. So, you sit there.

It's been weeks and you're alone. Not because they left you
Because you pushed. You don't want anyone around you
You're punishing yourself, can't you see it?
It's been weeks and you're not sleeping. Not because you're awake
Because you are exhausted. You can't turn you mind off these days
You're hurting yourself, can't you feel it?

And I wonder, am I doing the right thing by leaving you alone…
Sometimes the battle can't be won by other people.
When will you choose to stand?

I Know What You're Thinking

I know you think I will never find
Another guy like you,
And I'll just keep waiting for
You to be done playing with
The dolls and come home,
To the girl you love

I know you think I will never love
Any other guy that's not you,
And just keep waiting for
You to finally prove to me
That you love me
And are willing to show me

I know you think I will never leave
You for another guy,
And just keep watching life
Grow and wither around me
Seeing the dust settle as I wait
All alone for you

But I will not wait for you.

I know you will never find
Another girl like me,
Someone who loves you
Despite the faults and
Can anticipate your every move

Someone to come home to

I know you will never love
Another girl like me,
Someone who can put themselves
Aside for someone else
And learn to love again and again
Someone worth the wait

I know you will never leave
A girl like me alone
Because you like to feed off
My strength and yank the
Rod out of my back for yourself
Someone who's finally leaving…

You.
All alone.

Perfect Love

I am loved perfectly
There's Someone in my life who
Will never have enough of me
Who will not shout at me
And whose love is always the same

He keeps me safe from harm
And holds me on the long nights
Watches over me when I sleep
He catches every tear from my eyes
And He forgives me every time

I am loved perfectly with this love
The kind of love wars are waged for
The kind of love you hope in
The kind of love you search for
And I've already found it

There's no ups, no downs, no take backs or comebacks
There simply is a God who loves me
Perfectly, sincerely, and always
With a strength that never weakens

(Of Course I Love You Too)

Every now and then days of
Deep bleakness cloud our course
And sitting next to you, I
Cannot help but wonder if love
Will remain the ties connecting you
With me, and if love is strong enough too

Even in the conflict it remains true of
Me that I find you to be the course
On which my life is on, no matter where I
Go, you are always beside me, my love
As distant as we may find ourselves, you
Always come back to me, and I come back too

I'd tell you to not be scared of
Losing me, but I know of course
There are many meaningless words I
Use to help you see how much I love
You, the fear will remain all the same for you
I just want you to know that I'm scared too

I whisper softly in your ear, darling of
Mine, I'm here and I will stay the course.
I see that your heart fears what I
Do with this fragile heart of yours that I love
Trust me, I give my safety line to you
But I am quivering, I am petrified too

I step into your arms and gaze into eyes of
The oceans depths and reminding you that our course
Has not been easy or without trials but I
Have always found myself beside you, my love
For our love is not fragile and neither are you
I have another reminder for you too

One simple fact:
Of course I love you too.

Perspective

My Dear, have you ever seen yourself
Through my eyes?
Do you see what I see in you?
I cannot believe that you have,
Because if you saw yourself like I do,
Even just the slightest glimpse,
You'd fall hopelessly in love with you too

Enough

I love you
Can't that be enough?
Can't you take my word as
Collateral until I can show you?
I miss you
Still, not enough?
Isn't that an indicator of the
Ways that I need you?
Please let it be enough.
I don't have much else to give,
My heart's seen better days,
It's not worth much now.
But, if you wanted it from my
Rib cage, you could take it too
I don't need anything else back
Please, just take care of my love,
Care for the way I miss you
And care for my fragile heart.
I don't know if I'll ever
Have more than this to give.

Let Me

Paint me with flames.
Show me what it's like to be
Graffiti, brash and neon

Make me the beat of your soul
Sings when you're all alone,
Full of hopes and wishes

Let me be everything you love,
Let me show you how wonderful you are
At your depths: You are all I know to love.

I Found You

Home is your heartbeat
Home is the smell of your t-shirt wrapped around me
Home is your short laugh when surprise you and make you
laugh
Home is the sound of you singing to me in the car
Home is your fingers intertwined with me
Home is kisses on my fingers, pointedly on my ring finger
Home is when we hold each other when we cry
Home is being uncomfortably warm when we snuggle
Home is finding each other's lost things around the house
Home is adventures where I trail behind, but you always wait
for me
Home is movies where I ask too many questions and I stare
at you the whole time
Home is when you carry me over your shoulder because I'm
being stubborn
Home is long walks together and picnics in the sunshine
Home is our life together and the future that's coming
Home is what we will fill together with children and memories
Home is wherever we are
Home is in our hearts.

Our broken pieces fit together perfectly.

The Space in Between

Belief is soft
It builds like the pressure
In your lungs when you sing
Hugging you with a beloved
Flame ruining a debilitating day
Spin rhythmically and listen to the
Cosmos as they curve their graffiti
Around you, it's alive
Pivot in the nuanced air
Be free from the gloom and
 Paint your life without fear

Fasten With Me

Be my anchor.
Keep me grounded
So that I do not
Float away on the
Possibilities of life,

Be my glue.
Keep me stuck
Here in the few
Moments I
Have with you,

Be my knot.
Keep me bound
In the present because
We know
The past is a black hole,

I want to hold
Our memories by
The hand.

I want to affix
My gaze on
Our love.

I want to lock

Our two families
Together, I Do.

The way my heart
Adheres to yours
Is impossible to
Counterfeit

Let's brace ourselves
On each other
For this union
Shakes the earth

Let's stand united
Through the adversity
That seeks to
Drown our souls

Let's fasten onto love.

Cruise

Blurring past me goes my life,
All its colorful moments lump
Into an ostentatious abstract
Painting, in which I am the subject,

The girl lying in the field
Marveling at the Creator's work,
As her mind speeds among the stars
Traveling through the galaxies,

In search of you. When can I
Slow down? And just cruise along,
Enjoy the journey instead of
Looking ahead to the destination.

I want to be right here,
Looking next to me and seeing
You there, marveling along
With me, the wind whispers

Its words of encouragement
Through the silky tendrils combing
Through my hair, calming my
Racing heart, lulling me closer to you

The fear of setting this relationship

On cruise, is so strong and I pray
To The One Who Saves that I'll
Make it through without burns

My feelings are a cage that ensnare
My heart to yours. Will you feel the
Same that I do or will I be left to
Dream alone? I cannot bear it so.

Since the cruise button is within
My grasp and I know my fingers
Burn to push it like my heart
Burns for yours. Closer, closer still

It's not fair that we are young
That we may not know the full
Meaning of the three words that
I will never ever speak aloud

All I know is that everything
Could change in an instant
These feelings could grow or
Falter and so I'm putting on cruise

To enjoy my moments with you.

This Broken Voice Will Be Heard

I used to be defined by words that others said of me
I used to take on the burdens they pushed on me
I used to believe that I deserved it. And more.

But today, I stand before you defined by myself
Today, I stand before you, lighter than I've ever been
Today, I say that this broken voice of mine will be heard

I will not be quiet anymore.